Easter Journey

SUSIE POOLE

Dedicated to Phoebe Elizabeth
born 28 February 2004

pupfish

Published by Pupfish Limited
9 Brixton Avenue, Withington, Manchester M20 1JF
United Kingdom
www.pupfish.com

This book has been made using paper and board from sustainable resources.

A CIP catalogue record for this book is available from the British Library.
ISBN: 1-904637-02-7
ISBN: 1-904637-13-2

Printed and bound in China by Leo Paper Products

Easter Journey

SUSIE POOLE

How wonderful! The chill of winter is
coming to an end and at last the sun feels
warm on my face. Cheerful springtime
flowers are pushing up through the ground,
swaying in the sunshine. Bare, brown trees
are coming alive with fresh, green leaves.
After the dark and cold of winter,
how happy everything looks.

But new life is not just for flowers and trees.
It's for people too! This is where our
Easter Journey begins.

God had made his brand new world, and life was springing up everywhere. The sea was teeming with fish, the sky with birds, the land with plants wriggling up towards the warm sunshine. God made Adam and Eve, too. He made them to live forever. They sang at the top of their voices, ran across the plains, and walked and talked with their amazing Daddy, God.

There was so much for Adam and Eve to enjoy. For a while, all was perfect. But one day, Adam and Eve did the very thing God had asked them never to do. God was broken-hearted. He had to send them away, their perfect new life spoiled.

Adam and Eve had children, and so
their family grew, filling the Earth
with people. But everywhere people
lived, wickedness lived too.

God watched the people lying,
stealing and hurting each other.
They had forgotten about him.
He was sorry he had ever
made them.

But one man listened to
God – a good man, called
Noah. God told Noah he was
going to destroy the world
and make it new again.
He gave Noah plans for
an enormous boat. An ark.

"Build it exactly as I say,"
God said. "Then take two
of every animal and your
family, and get inside.
I will keep you safe."

Noah obeyed God. As the
door of the ark slammed
shut behind them, it began
to rain. It rained for forty
days and forty nights!
Soon, a deep and angry sea
covered the whole earth.
Outside, every person and
every animal was washed
away. Inside, Noah and his
family were safe and dry.

Finally, God stopped
the rain. Noah and his family
were so happy to be alive. God was
happy, too. He made a rainbow and
a promise. "There will never be
another flood like that!"

After many years,
the earth was filled with people again.

But did they remember God?

From Noah's family came a man called Abraham. He was God's special friend. He listened when God spoke and obeyed him. This made God very happy. "Abraham," God said. "You will be the father of a great big family. My special people, the Israelites!"

But even God's special people forgot about him and did bad things. They pretended God wasn't there, made other gods out of stone and wood, and knelt in front of them in worship!

There was no end to the trouble. God called what the people did sin.

"From now on," he said, "if any of you does something wrong, if anyone sins, you must bring a perfect animal to me. I will take the life of the animal in place of your life."

So the people tried very hard and brought their best animals to him. But God knew the animals weren't enough to save them from their sins forever. What could be done? God had a plan.

For a long, long time, God watched his people living on the earth. Always by his side was his Son.

Sometimes God spoke to his people through his friends, the prophets. "Don't worry," he told them, "a Saviour is coming who will help you and rescue you from your sin. He will give you new life."

The Saviour was to be God's precious, only Son.

At just the right time, God sent his Son to live on the earth. Leaving behind his beautiful, heavenly throne, he was born in a cold, smelly stable.

His mother Mary was just an ordinary village girl. His father Joseph was a carpenter. Mary and Joseph gave him the name Jesus – just as the angel, Gabriel, had told them.

That night, the skies rang with the songs of angels welcoming the Saviour to earth. Shepherds heard the good news and hurried into Bethlehem to worship baby Jesus. From a faraway land, wise men travelled to give precious gifts. Mary wondered if the gifts gave a clue about what her baby son would become.

As Jesus grew, he learned the ways of his earthly father, Joseph the carpenter. Jesus spent many hours in his workshop learning how to make something beautiful and useful from a rough piece of wood.

Jesus was learning the ways of his heavenly Father, too. At the temple, he listened to the words of the prophets and talked with the temple teachers. They were amazed by how much he understood, and realized he was very special.

It was in the temple that Jesus heard the words of Isaiah, one of the great prophets.

"He took all our suffering and pain. We saw how much it hurt him and thought that God was punishing him for something he had done wrong. But he was suffering because of the wrong things we have done. The punishment we should have had, God gave to him instead."

Isaiah 53

Jesus loved his heavenly Father and knew he had a special plan for him.

Some time later, when Jesus had grown up, there was great excitement in the land of Israel. John the Baptist thundered out of the desert with an amazing message from God:

"The Saviour is coming! Get ready! You need to say sorry for the bad things you've done. Then do what is right!"

Crowds of people came down to the river where John waited to baptize them. Down under the water the people went; up they came, leaving their sins behind them.

Suddenly, John stopped. He saw Jesus coming. John and Jesus used to play together as children. But now John knew that Jesus was the Saviour God had sent.

Jesus had come to be baptized, too. He knew this was part of God's plan. As he came up out of the water, the sky burst open. Like a dove, the Holy Spirit came down from heaven and rested on Jesus' head. As God's light glowed, the wonderful sound of his voice surrounded them.

"This is my son and **I love** him.
I am very pleased with him."

From that time on,
Jesus went everywhere
teaching about God.
He healed people too!

One day a blind man
lay crumpled by the
roadside.

"Jesus, help me!" he shouted.
Jesus was happy to help.
He made the man see again.

Jesus went to the house of
a little girl who had just
died. He pushed past
the weeping onlookers,
took her hand and said,
"It's time to get up!" And
so she did – alive and well,
ready for something to eat!

Great crowds began to follow Jesus everywhere he went. They wanted to be near him. They wanted to hear his words. They wanted more miracles.

Jesus chose twelve helpers, called disciples. The men stayed close to Jesus and saw for themselves how needy the people were. Jesus gathered them together and told them how to take care of the people for God.

There were others following Jesus, too; the Pharisees. These were the teachers of the Law of God, and they were worried about Jesus. They did not believe he was the Son of God. Mostly, they were jealous of him! People liked Jesus more than them.

The Pharisees didn't like Jesus' friends either. Jesus loved all kinds of people – grumpy people, dishonest people, rich people, poor people. He even loved very, very bad people. He wanted all of them to enjoy the new life God had for them.

Mary Magdalene was a woman who had lived a horrible life. The mistakes she had made were so, so big. But Jesus forgave her and was her friend.

When she came to see Jesus, the Pharisees muttered, "If he really was from God, he wouldn't even be seen with such an awful woman!" They began to hate Jesus. And they weren't the only ones. The leaders and priests from the temple all started thinking of ways to stop him.

Jesus knew exactly what these men were planning.
He knew God's plan too. So he warned his disciples.
"I'm going to suffer many things, and then I will be
killed," he said. "But don't be afraid. After three days,
I will come back to life."

The disciples did not understand. They did not want
Jesus to die.

Jesus could have hidden or run away. But he didn't!
He went to the city of Jerusalem, where all of these
men were gathered. He climbed onto a donkey and –
like a king in a parade – rode into the city.

His followers shouted happy praises to God.
They made a special path for him out of coats
and palm leaves.

"Hosanna," they shouted. "Save us."

"You are our king – sent by God!" they sang.

But not everyone felt this way.
The temple priests and leaders of
the people plotted and planned.
They looked for a way to kill Jesus.

One of Jesus' disciples, Judas, was greedy and cross. As the disciples came into the city, he went secretly to the temple priests and told them, "If you give me money, I will help you catch Jesus."

Jesus went to the upstairs room of a house in Jerusalem, where a special celebration feast had been prepared for him to eat with his friends. The disciples flopped around the table, tired from all the walking they had done.

Jesus took a bowl of water and knelt down in front of his disciples. He picked up each smelly, dirty foot and washed it. Peter was embarrassed. "No, Lord!" he said. "Don't wash my feet!" He could not let his Lord do a servant's job.

But Jesus said, "I must wash you. If I don't, you cannot share in my new life." So Peter put his foot back in the bowl. When Jesus finished he said, "I did this to show you how you should love and help each other. I want you to do the same."

Jesus and his disciples sat down to eat their special meal. While they were eating, Jesus took some bread. He said thank you to God for it, and then he broke it into pieces.

"This bread is like my body, which will be broken for you," Jesus said. Then he took a cup of wine. He thanked God and said, "Drink this, everyone, and remember my blood, which I will bleed for you."

The disciples did not understand. They still could not believe that Jesus was really going to die. But Jesus told them it was true. He even told them that he knew who would hand him over to the temple priests to be killed. It was one of them! The disciples looked at each other, wondering who it could be.

But Judas, knowing it was him, slipped silently through the door.

When the meal was finished, they sang a psalm together. The disciples were sad and very tired, but Jesus wanted them to go with him to the Garden of Gethsemane.

"I'm only going to be with you a little longer," Jesus said. He turned to Peter, James and John. "My heart feels so heavy, I am so unhappy. Please stay with me and pray."

Then Jesus went just a little way from them and fell onto the ground. He knew that the time was coming when he would be taken away from his friends, and worse still, from his Father in heaven. He knew that he would die a horrible death. "Please, Father," he prayed, "if there is another way, don't let this happen to me. But it's not what I want that is important. I will do what you want."

While he was praying, his friends had fallen asleep. He woke them up and said, "Look – they're coming to get me!"

Soldiers marched through the olive grove, Judas leading the way. Judas kissed Jesus on the cheek, pointing out that he was the one they wanted.

Peter tried to fight. But Jesus told him, "Put away your sword. Even this is part of God's plan."
The other disciples ran off into the darkness as fast as they could. They were very afraid.

The soldiers grabbed Jesus and led him to the temple priests, teachers of the law, and leaders of the people. When the high priest stood up and asked, "Are you the Saviour King, the Son of God?" Jesus said, "Yes, I am."

The people would not believe him. They shouted, and shook with anger. They hit Jesus and spat on him. Then they took him to the Roman governor of the land, Pilate. He had the power to have Jesus punished.

Meanwhile, the temple priests and leaders of the people had been busy in the city, spreading lies about Jesus. Now the same people who had loved him, wanted him dead.

Pilate did not think Jesus was guilty, but he could hear the crowd shouting, "Kill him! Kill Jesus!" Pilate was afraid of them and so he did as they asked.

Pilate's soldiers twisted together a crown of sharp thorns and jammed it on Jesus' head. "Look, everyone, it's King Jesus!" they laughed. They placed a heavy wooden cross on his back and made him carry it to a place outside the city.

Jesus was nailed to the cross – crucified. Two robbers hung on crosses beside him. Jesus looked down and saw the sneering faces of the soldiers and the crowd. He prayed, "Father, forgive them. They don't know what they're doing."

Suddenly all was still. Jesus' voice broke through the quiet, "My God, why have you left me alone?"

But Jesus was the perfect, sinless offering God needed. God would take Jesus' life in place of the sinful lives of all people. This was God's plan.

"It's all done," Jesus cried out. And at the moment Jesus died, the earth trembled and rocks cracked.

Jesus was buried in a tomb cut out of rock, and a huge stone was rolled in front of the opening.

Mary Magdalene was broken-hearted. Jesus had taken away her sins and given her new life. She missed him so much. So as soon as the sun came up on Sunday morning, she went to visit the tomb, taking with her special perfume and spices to put on his broken body.

But suddenly, as Mary got closer, the earth shook. A mighty angel flashed down from heaven and rolled away the stone! Presently, Mary arrived at the tomb. With horror, she peered into the darkness and saw that it was empty!

Where was Jesus?

"You won't find him here," said the angel. "But there is nothing to fear. He's alive! So go quickly and tell his disciples."

Full of wonder, Mary began to run. She was crying too. Crying and laughing. Running, crying and laughing – on her way to tell the disciples.

As Mary stumbled through the garden, she suddenly
came across a man that she thought was the gardener.
But this was no gardener.

"Mary," he said.

It was Jesus! She fell at his feet,
wanting to hold on to him tight
and not let go. But Jesus said,
"Don't hold on to me now.
Go and tell everyone
I am going to be with
my Father."

Later, Jesus appeared to his disciples. They were hiding behind locked doors. Tired and afraid. Suddenly, there Jesus stood, in the middle of the room, smiling at them! The disciples were overjoyed. They touched him to make sure he was really there and wasn't a ghost! Jesus showed them the holes in his hands, and the cut in his side.

"Go to every place in the world, near and far," he told them, "and tell people this: Whoever believes in me will be rescued from their sins. I will give them new life!"

Our Easter Journey has come to an end, but for those who believe the good news about Jesus, new life begins. A new start. All the bad things we've done, gone forever!

And this was God's plan. No more floods and animal sacrifices as in Noah's and Abraham's day. Instead, God loved us so much that he sent his son away from his home in heaven, to die on a cross and rescue us.

Now you know that Easter is not just about new life for flowers and trees, you can tell your friends, too. Easter is all about the new life Jesus gave to people just like you and me!

Thank you, Jesus.

GLOSSARY

BAPTIZE *dip someone in water. It is as if they leave wrong things behind in the water and come out washed clean, to start a new life*

CRUCIFY *kill a prisoner by nailing them to a cross made out of wood, and leaving them there until they die*

DISCIPLES *the twelve men Jesus chose to help him do his work*

FORGIVE *not punish someone who has done something wrong*

HOLY SPIRIT *the presence of God and the power he gives to people that belong to him.*

HOSANNA! *praise God!*

JERUSALEM *the most important city near to where Jesus lived*

LORD *a name for Jesus; it means "master". He is in charge of everything that God has made*

MIRACLE *God doing something in an amazing or unexpected way*

OFFERING *a gift*

PHARISEES *a group of men who knew all the rules and laws, and were careful to keep every single one*

PRIEST

someone who helped people to worship God

PROPHET

someone who had a special message from God for other people

PSALM

a song to God, usually giving thanks or praise. The Book of Psalms in the Bible has 150 songs in it

ROMAN GOVERNOR

Roman leader in Jerusalem, called Pilate. The Romans ruled the country where Jesus lived

SACRIFICE

kill an animal as an offering to God, to say thank you or sorry to him

SAVIOUR

someone who rescues people

SIN

something we do, think or say that God doesn't want us to do

TEMPLE

a building where people went to worship God

TOMB

the place where someone's body was buried when they died

WORSHIP

the way we let God know how much we love him and say thank you for what he has done

pupfish

inspired books & music for children

Pupfish books are making a splash by creating beautiful books for children that are more than just a good read. Each book dives deep into the bible for inspiration, and surfaces with treasure that will open the child's mind, heart and spirit to the wonders of God and His amazing world.

To take a closer look at Pupfish, and for a full list of titles and other products visit:

www.pupfish.com